AMAZING SCIENCE

FORCES AND MOVEMENT

Sally Hewitt

WAYLAND

Published in paperback in 2014 by Wayland

Wayland
Hachette Children's Books
338 Euston Road, London NW1 3BH

Senior Editor: Joyce Bentley
Senior Design Manager: Rosamund Saunders
Designer: Tall Tree

British Library Cataloguing in Publication Data
Hewitt, Sally,
Forces and Movement - (Amazing Science)
1. Force and energy - Juvenile literature
2. Movement - Juvenille literature
I. Title
531.1'1

ISBN: 978-0-7502-8055-6

Printed and bound in China

10 9 8 7 6 5 4 3 2 1

Cover photograph: Male athletes at a finishing line. Alan Thornton/Getty Images
Title page: A T Willet/Getty Images

Photo credits: David Ducros/Science Photo Library 6, Corbis 7, Altrendo Images/Getty Images 8, Brooke Slezak/Getty Images 9, David Madison/Getty Images 10, Didier Givois/Getty Images 11, Alan Thornton/Getty Images 12, Southern Stock/Getty Images 13, Bill Ross/Corbis 14, Phil Banko/Getty Images 15, Ray Massey/Getty images 16, Florida Images/Alamy 17, David Woolley/Getty Images 18, Steffen Thalemann/Getty Images 19, Randy Faris/Corbis 20, Simon Watson/Getty Images 21, Joe McBride/Getty Images 22, Shogoro/Getty Images 23, Leslie Garland Picture Library/Alamy 24, Andy Crawford/Getty Images 25, A T Willet/Getty Images 26 Hubert Stadler/Corbis 27.

Contents

Amazing forces

...5, 4, 3, 2, 1 blast off! A huge blast pushes a space rocket away from Earth out into space.

A force is a push or a pull that makes things move.

A push or a pull can make things move up, down, backwards, forwards or round and round.

A man is pushing his daughter on the swing.

YOUR TURN!

Make a ball and a toy car move in different ways. Did you give it a push or a pull?

SCIENCE WORDS: force move

Push and pull

A snowplough is a big, powerful machine. It has a strong metal bucket to push and lift enormous loads.

The snowplough moves forward and pushes the snow in front of it.

Pushing is the opposite to pulling. You pull a sledge along behind you.

YOUR TURN!

Put on and take off some gloves. Are you giving them a push, a pull or both?

A sledge moves easily over slippery snow.

SCIENCE WORDS: push pull

Moving along

A racing car speeds along the track. Its powerful engine makes a loud, roaring type of sound.

The engine makes a strong force that pushes the car forwards.

Bikes don't have an engine. You have to push the pedals to make the wheels turn.

YOUR TURN!

What moves along on wheels? What force turns the wheels?

The force of your legs moves the bike.

SCIENCE WORDS: engine pedals wheels

Running fast

Sprinters are the fastest runners in the world. They need a lot of strength and power to run so fast.

Runners have strong muscles to power them along.

Muscles pull your bones when you move. Strong muscles help you to run faster and jump higher.

YOUR TURN!

Hold your top left arm with your right hand. Move your left arm. Feel the muscle pulling the bones in your arm.

Exercise helps to keep your muscles strong.

SCIENCE WORDS: fast muscles

Start and stop

Eurostar is a high speed train. It speeds over the ground and under the sea between London and Paris.

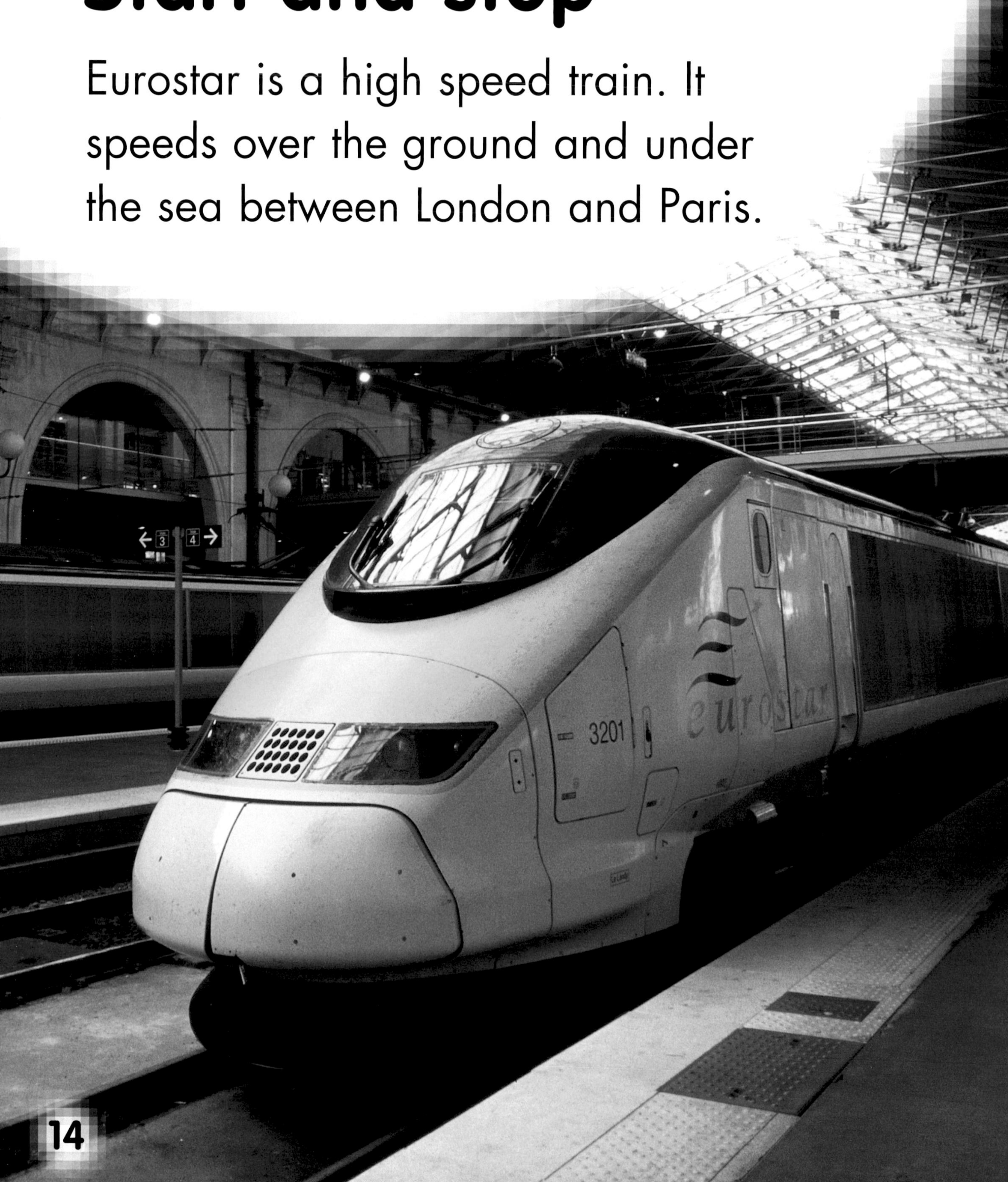

The driver uses the controls to start, move and stop the train. It slows down and stops at the station.

Computers tell the driver how fast the train is going.

WARNING!

Moving traffic is dangerous. Stop, look and listen. Make sure there is no traffic coming before you start to cross the road.

The train speeds along straight tracks. It slows down on winding tracks.

SCIENCE WORDS: start stop slow

Rubbing together

A shark is a good shape for swimming fast. It has a smooth, pointed shape to cut through water.

Water and air rub against anything that moves through them and slows them down.

When things rub together they make a force called friction. Friction slows things down.

YOUR TURN!

Push a toy car along over carpet and over a smooth floor. What happens?

The toy car's wheels **rub** against the carpet. It slows down and stops.

SCIENCE WORDS: rub friction

Changing shape

Pizza cooks toss, flatten, push and pull dough. They use their hands to make it into a flat, round shape.

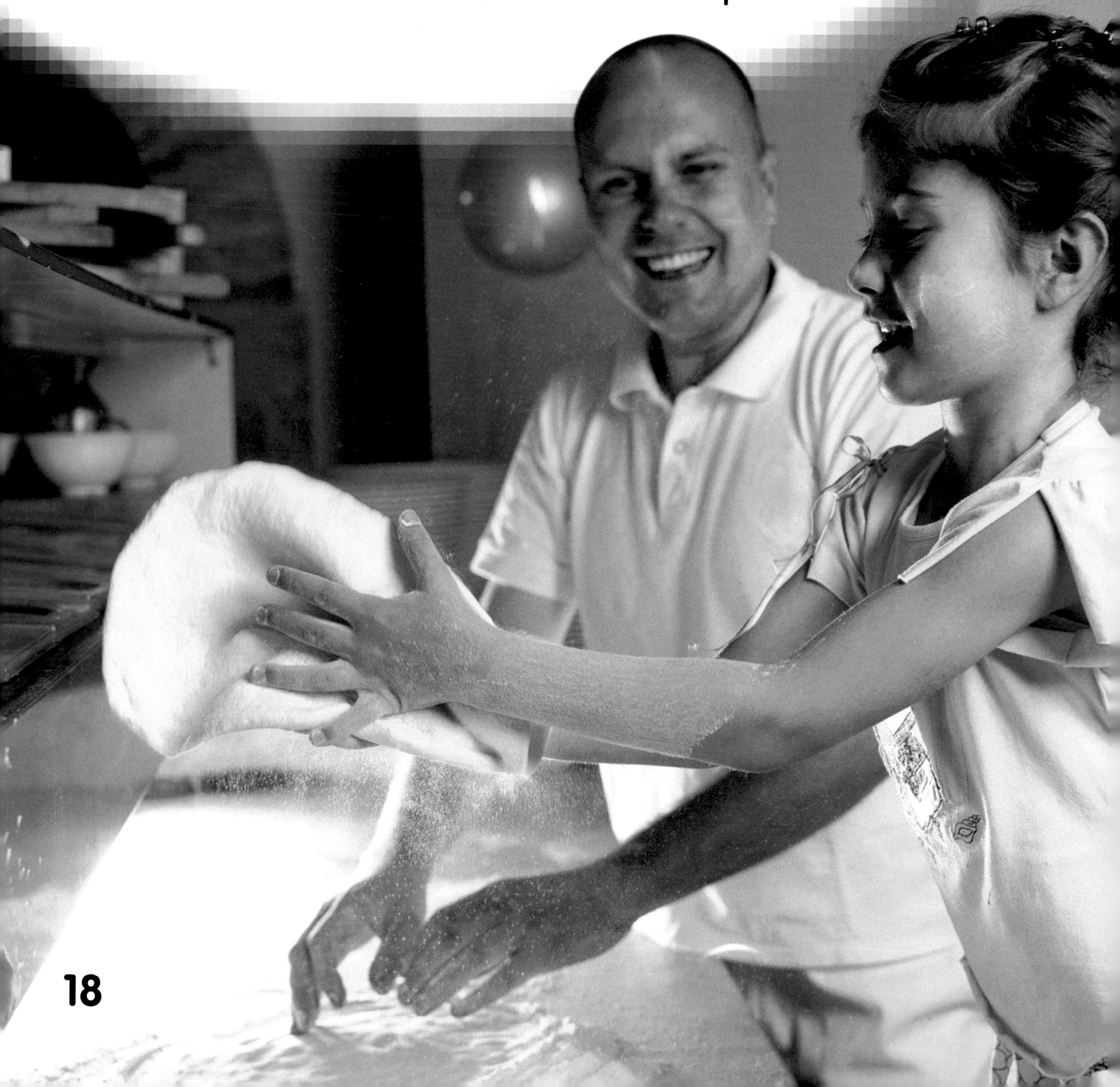

Pushes and pulls change the shape of squashy, stretchy materials such as dough.

When you blow air into a balloon, it changes shape.

YOUR TURN!

Push, pull, squash and stretch modelling clay to make new shapes.

Blowing pushes air into the stretchy balloon.

SCIENCE WORDS: change shape

Elastic and springs

A bungee jumper dives off a tall crane. An elastic cord stops her falling and bounces her back up again.

Elastic material stretches when you pull it. It snaps back into shape when you let it go.

A spring in a pogo stick squashes when you push it down.

The spring pushes back up to make you bounce.

YOUR TURN!

Push down on a stapler. Let go and watch how springs inside make it jump open.

SCIENCE WORDS: elastic spring

Falling

A skydiver jumps from an aeroplane and falls through the air. Gravity pulls the skydiver down to the ground.

Things fall down because of a natural force called gravity.

Air pushes up on the parachute and slows the skydiver's fall.

YOUR TURN!

Drop a piece of paper. How does it fall? Now crumple it and drop it again. How does it fall now?

The parachute stops the diver from hurting himself when he hits the ground.

SCIENCE WORDS: **gravity** **fall**

Magnets

A giant magnet on a crane pulls iron towards it with a strong force called magnetism.

Things made of iron are magnetic. A magnet pulls and moves magnetic things.

A magnet cannot pick up things made of plastic, wool or wood.

YOUR TURN!

Collect things made of metal, plastic and wood. Use a magnet. What will it pull, move and pick up?

Metal paperclips stick to a magnet.

SCIENCE WORDS: magnet iron magnetism

Wind and water

A tornado is a swirling tube of wind. It is strong enough to knock down large buildings and houses.

Wind is moving air. You can feel it pushing against you.

Flowing water is a strong force. It pushes against things and moves them along.

YOUR TURN!

Fly a kite. Feel the wind push it up in the air.

The force of water pushes a water wheel round.

SCIENCE WORDS: wind water

Glossary

Change
When you change something, you make it different.

Engine
An engine gives cars, tractors, trains and aeroplanes the power they need to move.

Elastic
Elastic stretches when you pull it and snaps back when you let it go.

Fall
An object will fall down when you drop it.

Fast
Moving fast is moving very quickly. It is the opposite to slow.

Force
A force is a push or a pull that makes things move.

Friction
When things rub together they make a force called friction.

Gravity
Gravity is a force that pulls things down towards the ground.

Iron
Iron is a kind of metal.

Magnet
A magnet pulls things made of iron towards it with a force called magnetism.

Magnetism
A natural force. A magnet pulls metal objects towards it with magnetism.

Move
When you move you aren't still. Pushes and pulls make things move.

Muscles
Your muscles push and pull your bones when you move.

Pedals
You push pedals on a bike to turn the wheels and make the bike move.

Pull
You pull something towards you to make it move or change shape.

Push
You push something away from you to make it move or change shape.

Rub
You rub a mirror with a cloth to clean it. You rub your hands together to make them warm.

Shape
A ball has a round shape. A snake has a long, thin shape.

Slow
Not moving quickly. Slow is the opposite of fast.

Spring
A spring is a coil that squashes when you push down on it and springs back up when you let it go.

Start
To start is to begin. Something starts to move when it is given a push or a pull.

Stop
To stop moving is to be still.

Water
Flowing water is a force that can make things move.

Wheels
A wheel is round. Cars and trucks move along on turning wheels.

Wind
Wind is moving air.

Index